40 DAYS THROUGH THE BOOK

STUDY GUIDE + STREAMING VIDEO
SIX SESSIONS

ROMANS

IN THE GRIP OF GRACE

MAX LUCADO

WITH KEVIN & SHERRY HARNEY

HarperChristian
Resources

40 Days Through the Book: Romans Study Guide
© 2021 by Max Lucado

Requests for information should be addressed to: HarperChristian Resources, 3900 Sparks Dr. SE, Grand Rapids, Michigan 49546

ISBN 978-0-310-14602-5 (softcover)
ISBN 978-0-310-14603-2 (ebook)

HarperChristian Resources titles may be purchased in bulk for church, business, fundraising, or ministry use. For information, please e-mail ResourceSpecialist@ChurchSource.com.

The themes of this study are drawn from the video study of the same name by Max Lucado. All other resources, including the session introductions, small group discussion questions, prayer direction, and the 40 Days learning and reflection exercises and have been written by Kevin and Sherry Harney in collaboration with Max Lucado.

First printing February 2021 / Printed in the United States of America

25 26 27 28 29 LBC 8 7 6 5 4

CONTENTS

HOW TO USE THIS GUIDE

SCOPE AND SEQUENCE

Welcome to the *40 Days Through the Book* study on Romans. During the course of the next six weeks, you will embark on an in-depth exploration of Paul's message to the church in Rome. During this study, you will learn when Paul wrote the book, the audience for whom it was written, and the background and context in which it was written. But, more importantly, through the teaching by Max Lucado, you will explore the key themes that Paul relates in the book—and how his teachings relate to you today.

SESSION OUTLINE

The *40 Days Through the Book* video and study guide are designed to be experienced in a group setting (such as a Bible study, Sunday school class, or other small-group gathering) and also as an individual study. Each session begins with an introductory reading and question. You will then watch the video message, which can be accessed through streaming by following the instructions printed on the inside front cover. There is an outline provided in the guide for you to take notes and gather your reflections as you watch the video.

Next, you will engage in a time of directed discussion, review the memory verse for the week, and then close each session with a time of prayer. (Note that if you are doing this study with others and your group is larger, you may wish to watch the videos together and then break into smaller groups of four to six people, to ensure that everyone has time to participate in discussions.)

40-DAY JOURNEY

What is truly unique about this study, and the other studies in the *40 Days Through the Book* series, are the daily learning resources that will lead you into a deeper engagement with the text. Each week, you will be given a set of daily readings, with accompanying reflection questions, to help you explore the material that you covered during your group time.

The first day's reading will focus on the key verse to memorize for the week. In the other weekly readings, you will be invited to read a passage from the book of Romans, reflect on the text, and then respond with some guided journal questions. On the final day, you will review the key verse again and recite it from memory. As you work through the six weeks' worth of material in this section, you will read (and, in some cases, reread) the entire book of Romans.

Now, you may be wondering why you will be doing this over the course of *forty* days. Certainly, there is nothing special about that number. But there is something biblical about it. In the Bible, the number forty typically designates a time of *testing*. Noah was in the ark for forty days. Moses lived forty years in Egypt and another forty years in the desert before he led God's people. He spent forty days on Mount Sinai receiving God's laws and sent spies, for forty days, to investigate the land of Canaan. Later, God sent the prophet Jonah to warn ancient Nineveh, for forty days, that its destruction would come because of the people's sins.

Even more critically, in the New Testament we read that Jesus spent forty days in the wilderness, fasting and praying. It marked a critical transition point in his ministry—the place where he set about to fulfill the mission that God had intended. During this time Jesus was tested relentlessly by the enemy . . . and prevailed. When he returned to Galilee, he was a different person than the man who had entered into the wilderness forty days before. The same will be true for you as you commit to this forty-day journey through Romans.

GROUP FACILITATION

If you are doing this study with others, you and your fellow group members should have your own copy of this study guide. Not only will this help you engage when your group is meeting, but it will also allow you to fully enter into the *40 Days* learning experience. Keep in mind the video, questions, and activities are simply tools to help you engage with the session. The real power and life-transformation will come as you dig into the Scriptures and seek to live out the truths you learn along the way.

You will need to appoint a leader or facilitator for the group who is responsible for starting the video teaching and for keeping track of time during discussions and activities. Leaders may also read questions aloud and monitor discussions, prompting participants to respond and ensuring that everyone has the opportunity to participate. For more thorough instructions on this role, see the Leader's Guide included at the back of this guide.

INTRODUCTION

ROMANS

AUTHOR, DATE, AND LOCATION

The apostle Paul wrote this letter to the church in Rome c. AD 57, almost three decades after the resurrection of Jesus and the birth of the Church. It is fair to say that Rome was the "center" of the world in the days of Paul. The most famous poets, politicians, philosophers, and people came from Rome, moved to Rome, or longed to visit this influential city. Paul knew that if the gospel grew healthy roots in Rome, it could spread all over the world. If the church in Rome was gripped by the grace of God, it could influence and help believers far and wide.

THE BIG PICTURE

Some of Paul's letters were written to dear friends, others to people he had mentored, and still others to churches that knew him well. The letter to the church in Rome was different. It was written to a group of believers who had not met Paul and were actually a bit cautious about him. He was a controversial person they had heard about but did not know personally. Paul's hope was to visit the believers in Rome on his way to Spain. So, as a preamble to their meeting, Paul sent a letter that was inspired by the Holy Spirit and came from deep within his heart. Romans is one of the richest theological works ever penned, yet it is also deeply personal.

The first eleven chapters focus with laser precision on the core beliefs of the Christian faith. If a believer wants to dig into the central teaching of the Bible, almost all of the core doctrines can be found in the book of Romans. The theme of these chapters is correct belief, or what theologians would call *orthodoxy*. Paul is showing the Roman church that his beliefs were absolutely in line with the Scriptures and the teaching of Jesus.

Starting in chapter twelve, there is a shift. With one word, the focus moves from belief to action. When Paul declares "Therefore," in Romans 12:1, he turns the reader's attention to what scholars call *orthopraxy*, or right Christian living. Once we know what we believe, we can move into action and daily behavior that honors and glorifies God.

In this one letter, Paul shows the Roman church that his beliefs and practices are unquestionably in line with the truth they have been taught. He gives a Spirit-breathed clarification of what the gospel is and how Jesus' people are to think and live in the grip of God's amazing grace. Paul, with authentic clarity and deep transparency, thus goes from being a controversial stranger to the Romans to a brother and friend—before they ever meet him.

Paul's words to the Romans contained the power to save souls, shape minds, and transform lives for the glory of Jesus. The exciting thing is that reading this book of the Bible can still do all of these things today! So brace yourself as you read this letter from Paul.

EPIC THEMES

There are several themes in Romans that are worthy of our focus. Some of these include:

- **The reality, danger, and power of sin.** Sin is the deepest problem that human beings face and has eternal consequences (see Romans 1-2).

- **God's grace is real, amazing, and available to all people.** Through Jesus, every person is invited to enter a relationship with the Father and be cleansed of their sin (see Romans 3-5).

- **God has broken our chains and set us free, but the battle with sin continues.** Our old way of life is dead and we are alive in Jesus, but the process of spiritual growth and becoming like Jesus takes a lifetime and demands continual surrender to the will and ways of God (see Romans 6-8).

- **God's beautiful story comes in four movements: creation, fall, redemption, and restoration.** We are part of a spiritual family tree that spans the Old and New Testaments in the Bible. God is engrafting us into a bigger story and family than we can imagine (see Romans 9-11).

- **Christians follow in the steps of their Savior.** This means that we walk the pathway of love. In a world driven by selfish ambition and self-centered demands, we humbly serve and sacrificially love others (see Romans 12–13).

- **Followers of Jesus are like passengers on a ship.** We are all on the same journey. We are part of an amazing family of faith, and God calls us to live in fellowship with each other (see Romans 14–16).

In the first eleven chapters of the book of Romans, the apostle Paul lays out the core beliefs of the Christian faith with clarity and precision. Then, in the final five chapters, Paul reveals how to live in ways consistent with those beliefs. So, as you start this journey, ask God to help you *understand* your faith at a deeper level than you ever have before, and then pray for the courage and strength to *live out* what you learn in your daily life. In addition, ask the Holy Spirit to help you understand God's grace, walk in that grace, and share it freely with every person you meet.

THE PROBLEM WE FACE

ROMANS 1–2

There is a problem that every human being faces called sin. It leads to consequences that are bigger than we realize. Try as we might, we can't solve this problem on our own. Thankfully, God has a solution, and he desires to deal with our sin.

WELCOME

When you look at the top-grossing movies of all time, there is one fascinating common trait that stands out: *heroes!* From the *Star Wars* movies to the *Lord of the Rings* trilogy to the *Avengers* franchise, about 60 percent of the top movies are stories of heroes. Even *The Ten Commandments*, which was made in 1956, shows up in the top ten-grossing movies of all time and presents Moses as a type of hero—and God as the ultimate hero.

All of this raises the question as to why we people are so drawn to heroes. But before we can answer that question, we first have to consider what a hero is. One simple definition is, "A person who is admired or idealized for courage, outstanding achievements, or noble qualities." In movies, these characters tend to do things that are far and above what "ordinary" people could or would choose to do. A war hero rushes back into battle to drag injured soldiers out of harm's way. A superhero flies in to save the day, or summons sea creatures to do their bidding, or throws a massive hammer that returns to their hand after defeating their enemies.

We are drawn to heroes because they have the courage, noble qualities, and power to change the world that we desire for our own lives. We admire these traits because they are rare in this world today. In fact, most of us would likely say we have never met a true hero.

Or have we?

If a hero is truly someone who lives with courage, achieves great things, and does that which is noble, then maybe we have met more heroes than we have recognized. When a person loves Jesus and follows his will, he or she might just qualify as a hero. Maybe your prayer-warrior grandmother was a hero. Maybe that faithful Sunday school teacher who opened the Bible and shared with middle school kids for three decades was a hero. Perhaps ordinary people who dare to follow God and obey his Word can become heroes.

Movies are nice, but what we need to see in this life are *real* people who live heroically as they follow Jesus, the ultimate hero. As we begin our forty-day journey through the book of Romans, we meet such a hero in the apostle Paul. His devotion to Jesus, his boldness to speak (and write) the truth, and his understanding of God's grace all serve as examples that we can seek to follow as we walk through the book of Romans.

SHARE

Think about the definition of a hero as being someone who has lived courageously with outstanding achievements and noble qualities. Who is someone you know who has lived such a heroic life? What is it about this person that makes them a hero in your eyes?

WATCH

Watch the video for session one. (Play the DVD or see the instructions on the inside front cover on how to access the sessions through streaming.) As you watch, use the following outline to record any thoughts or concepts that stand out to you.

Paul, an unusual but true hero (Romans 1:1–2)

Setting the scene: a prelude to a visit from Paul

A clear presentation of Christian doctrine from an unlikely source

The bad news first: the reality of sin and wrath (Romans 1:18–20)

How do we respond to sin?

Hedonism: pretending God does not exist (Romans 1:18–23)

Judgmentalism: ignoring our sinfulness and condemning others (Romans 2:1–3)

Legalism: trying to use religion to earn our way to God
(Romans 2:17–29)

The bottom line: *grace!*

DISCUSS

Take a few minutes with your group members to discuss what
you just watched and explore these concepts in Scripture. Use
the following questions to help guide your discussion.

1. What impacted you the most as you watched Max's teaching on Romans 1–2?

2. Paul was profoundly aware of his sins and broken past. Why is awareness of our need for grace so critical if we are going to have sound biblical beliefs (theology)?

3. Max described the suit of good deeds and religious works he wore for many years. How would you describe a garment of self-righteousness you wore before you came to really understand the good news of the grace of Jesus?

4. **Read Romans 1:21–32.** What are some of the consequences that a person faces who lives as a hedonist (as if God does not exist)?

5. **Read Romans 2:1–4.** What are signs or indicators that we are focusing on the sins of others while ignoring our own failings? Why is this so dangerous?

6. **Read Romans 2:17–24.** If we compare ourselves to people who are living deep in sin and are rebellious toward God, how can this bolster a false sense of self-righteousness? If we compare ourselves to Jesus, what does this do to our arrogance and self-reliance?

MEMORIZE

In each session, you will be given a key verse (or verses) from the passage covered in the video teaching to memorize. This week, your memory verse is from Romans 1:16:

> *For I am not ashamed of the gospel, because it is the power of God that brings salvation to everyone who believes: first to the Jew, then to the Gentile.*

Have everyone recite this verse out loud. Then go around the room again and have everyone try to say the verse completely from memory.

RESPOND

What will you take away from this session? What is a practical next step you can take that will move you toward fully embracing the grace of Jesus rather than being hedonistic, judgmental, or legalistic? Take a few moments to write down your thoughts.

PRAY

Close your group time by praying in any of the following directions:

- Ask God to forgive you for the times you have pursued your own hedonistic desires and forgotten to surrender to God's will for your life.
- Ask for the power of the Holy Spirit to help you stop judging others and look honestly at the need for repentance in your own heart and life.
- Pray for freedom from legalism and for deep understanding of God's grace in your life.

SESSION ONE

Reflect on the material you have covered in this session by engaging in the following between-session learning resources. Each week, you will begin with a day to preview the biblical theme from the session. During the next five days, you will have an opportunity to read a portion of Romans, reflect on what you learn, respond by taking action, journal some of your insights, and pray about what God has taught you. Finally, on the last day, you will review the epic theme of the session, reflect on what you have learned, and review how it has impacted your life.

DAY 1

Memorize: Begin this week's personal study by reciting Romans 1:16:

> For I am not ashamed of the gospel, because it is the power of God that brings salvation to everyone who believes: first to the Jew, then to the Gentile.

Now try to say the verse completely from memory.

Reflect: What does this tell you about the power of the gospel in your life?

DAY 2

Read: Romans 1:1–17.

Reflect: Among other things, the book of Romans is an introduction of the apostle Paul to the Christians in the city of Rome. If all you knew about Paul was found in these opening seventeen verses of the letter, what would you learn about his heart, relationship to Jesus, and care for God's church? Think about how you would picture Paul after reading these words.

Journal:
- As you read Romans 1:16–17, what do you learn about the gospel?

- Our faith is central to the gospel. What do you learn about the place of faith in this passage? How is your faith growing (if indeed it is)?

Pray: Ask for the power of the Holy Spirit to help you live by faith every moment of the day.

DAY 3

Read: Romans 1:18–32.

Reflect: As you read Romans 1:18–32, notice the recurring line in verses 24, 26, and 28: "God gave them over." It paints a picture of a downward spiral deeper and deeper into sin. What does this spiral look like in our world? In your own life?

Journal:
- Why do you think God, who loves us and wants us to be gripped by his grace, would give us over to our sin and allow us to keep running from him?

- What can you do to break the pattern of this downward spiral in your own life?

Pray: Confess where you see yourself running into sin and resisting God. Ask for power to turn back to God.

DAY 4

Read: Romans 2:1–16.

Reflect: We are all tempted to wear the judge's robe and spend too much time focusing on the sins and problems of other people. Think about your attitude toward others. What are some ways you can identify that you sit as "judge and jury"?

Journal:
- Why is God opposed to you and me sitting as the judge over other people?

- What are two or three ways that you tend to have a judgmental attitude?

Pray: Ask for forgiveness for any judgmental attitudes and actions and pray for eyes to see others the way God does.

DAY 5

Read: Romans 2:17–29.

Reflect: In the days of the apostle Paul, there were many people who lived with spiritual pride, religious arrogance, and bloated egos. The temptation to be a legalist and glory in our own "super spirituality" still exists today. Think back over the past week and take note of times that your attitudes, actions, or words were legalistic. What can you do to show more grace and respond with a less legalistic attitude toward others?

Journal:
- What were some of the legalistic and spiritually arrogant attitudes in the lives of the people to whom Paul was writing?
- What are some of the patterns of religious pride and legalism that can capture the heart of a Christian today? Reflect on your own life to make sure you are not exhibiting any of these patterns.

Pray: Ask the Holy Spirit to show you where legalism or religious arrogance has crept into your heart.

DAY 6

Read: Romans 2:21–32.

Reflect: We are messed up because of sin, and God wants to make us whole and healthy. This is the epic theme of these opening chapters of Romans. If we miss the truth that sin is more prevalent and dangerous than we think, we have not read this passage closely enough. If we begin to see the greatness of God's grace and willingness to deal with our sin, we are starting to get the big message. What is one step you can take in your own life to stop the downward spiral of sin pictured in this passage?

Journal:
- How do these chapters in Romans open your eyes to the reality of sin and the vastness of God's grace?
- Write a brief prayer of thanks for the gift of grace God has lavished on you.

Pray: Thank God that sin does not have the final word, but that his grace is greater than all our sins.

DAY 7

Memorize: Conclude this week's personal study by again reciting Romans 1:16:

> *For I am not ashamed of the gospel, because it is the power of God that brings salvation to everyone who believes: first to the Jew, then to the Gentile.*

Now try to say the verse completely from memory.

Reflect: What does God's gift of salvation mean to you personally?

THE GIFT WE'VE BEEN OFFERED

ROMANS 3–5

The God of heaven offers us the greatest gift imaginable: himself. God solved our sin problem by offering the gift of his own life. He sentenced himself for our sins and paid a price we never could. God's holiness is honored. Our sin is punished. And we are offered redemption.

WELCOME

All people in all places and at all times love a good gift. Children look forward to birthday parties because they know they will receive gifts from their friends. Mothers look forward to Mother's Day, and fathers to Father's Day, because they know their children have prepared something special for them. We all look forward to Christmas Day, the greatest gift-giving season of all, because of the excitement surrounding the packages under the tree.

There is a universal joy that comes with giving and receiving gifts. Sure, the gift list may change across the decades. In the 1970s, the Atari 2600, Pet Rocks, Rubik's cube, Weebles, Rock 'em Sock 'em Robots, and Lite-Brites were popular. The 1980s brought us Masters of the Universe action figures, Teddy Ruxpin, Big Wheels, and Bristle Blocks. In the 1990s, it was all about video games, the Discman, Doc Martens, and Beanie Babies.

As time passes, all gifts seem to go out of style. No one will be standing in line for half a day to get a Tickle Me Elmo this Christmas. Most people have caught on that paying good money for a rock in a box is not a wise investment. Fads come and go—and gifts break and eventually end up in the trash.

The good news is that there is a gift that our Father in heaven offers that is eternal, unbreakable, and never goes out of style. This gift is available to everyone. It is of infinite worth but is given freely. As the apostle Paul reveals in this next section of Romans, this free gift from God has a name . . . Jesus. "Righteousness is *given* through faith in Jesus Christ to all who believe . . . for all have sinned and fall short of the glory of God, and all are justified *freely* by his grace through the redemption that came by Christ Jesus" (Romans 3:22–24, emphasis added).

SHARE

Take a few minutes to go around the group and share any insights you have from last week's personal study. Then think about one of the most memorable gifts you ever received at a birthday, or at Christmas, or at some other gathering. What made that gift so memorable?

WATCH

Watch the video for session two. (Play the DVD or see the instructions on the inside front cover on how to access the sessions through streaming.) As you watch, use the following outline to record any thoughts or concepts that stand out to you.

The heart of our heavenly Father

The greatest gap in the world: the reality and severity of sin (Romans 3:13–16, 23–24)

The greatest hope in the world: the light of Jesus and the gift of grace (Romans 3:21–26)

Justification: being made righteous

Three arguments against grace (then and now):

Argument #1: It is too *risky* to be true (Romans 3:31)

Argument #2: It is too *new* to be true (Romans 4:1–2)

Argument #3: It is too *good* to be true (Romans 5:1–21)

An ancient story of grace: Abraham and Sarah

DISCUSS

Take a few minutes with your group members to discuss what you just watched and explore these concepts in Scripture. Use the following questions to help guide your discussion.

1. What impacted you the most as you watched Max's teaching on Romans 3–5?

2. **Read Romans 3:11–18.** How does Paul describe the extent of our sin? How do you see the reality of these words as you look at the world today?

3. **Read Romans 3:21–26.** As you read these verses, how do they bring hope, light, and life to you? How do they reveal the amazing grace of God?

4. Paul was concerned that if people realized they were *not* saved by works or by following the Old Testament law, they might decide *not* to follow God's laws or do good works. Why is Paul's concern legitimate? How do people today take advantage of God's grace?

5. Imagine someone tells you that they can't embrace the message of God's grace because it seems too good to be true. How would you explain the gift of Jesus is both amazingly good but also something they should receive and gladly accept as soon as possible?

6. Jesus offers to pay off *all* our debt—past, present, and future. How should our daily lives change when we live each moment aware of this amazing gift?

MEMORIZE

Your memory verses for this week are from Romans 3:23–24:

For all have sinned and fall short of the glory of God, and all are justified freely by his grace through the redemption that came by Christ Jesus.

Have everyone recite these verses out loud. Then go around the room again and have everyone try to say the verses completely from memory.

RESPOND

What is one area in your life in which you need to live more in the truth that Jesus has paid all your debt in full? How can your group members pray with you as you move forward living more fully in this truth? Take a few moments to write down your thoughts.

PRAY

Close your group time by praying in any of the following directions:

- Ask God to help you take the gift of Jesus seriously and never abuse his grace. Confess where you have taken the gift of grace too lightly.
- Thank God that the message of his grace is nothing new, but it has saturated how God has moved in the lives of his people from the beginning of time.
- Lift up prayers of praise that God's grace and the gift of Jesus are absolutely true, even though they may seem too good to be true.

SESSION TWO

Reflect on the material you have covered in this session by engaging in the following between-session learning resources. Each week, you will begin with a day to preview the biblical theme from the session. During the next five days, you will have an opportunity to read a portion of Romans, reflect on what you learn, respond by taking action, journal some of your insights, and pray about what God has taught you. Finally, on the last day, you will review the epic theme of the session, reflect on what you have learned, and review how it has impacted your life.

DAY 8

Memorize: Begin this week's personal study by reciting Romans 3:23–24:

> *For all have sinned and fall short of the glory of God, and all are justified freely by his grace through the redemption that came by Christ Jesus.*

Now try to say these verses completely from memory.

Reflect: What has Jesus done that makes him worthy of you placing your faith fully in him?

DAY 9

Read: Romans 3:1–20.

Reflect: It is easy to read a passage and think about how it applies to *others* while not reflecting on how it applies to *you*. As you read through this passage, let this simple truth sink in: *these words are talking about your favorite grandparent, your pastor, the greatest saint you know, and every person who has walked this earth . . . including you.* Only Jesus is exempt. Ponder this reality: every human being is under the power of sin without Jesus. What are some ways that sin has crept into your life in this past season?

Journal:
- What are some of the realities of sin you have to face if you are going to have a clear picture of grace?
- Why is it important for you to recognize that each declaration about sin in this passage applies to you?

Pray: Confess your sins to God and thank him that grace has been made fully available to you through the sacrifice of Jesus.

DAY 10

Read: Romans 3:21–31.

Reflect: We are saved by God's grace through faith, not by obeying the law. So, we can't boast or brag about this amazing gift that we have been offered. It is a gift, not something we have earned or worked to attain. Take time to search your heart and identify anywhere spiritual pride has crept in. Have you developed any patterns of spiritual boasting that you need to root out? How can you better seek to notice God's grace in your life with each passing day?

Journal:
- What are some of the rules and regulations Christians follow that can become a source of spiritual pride? Why does God give us warnings about this kind of behavior?
- Following God's law does not save us. But those who have received the grace of God and placed their faith in Jesus actually uphold the law of God joyfully. What are ways you can uphold and follow the teachings of the Bible—but do it with a clear understanding that your actions are a response to grace and not an effort to get it?

Pray: Thank God that all people, from every walk of life, can come to Jesus in exactly the same way: by placing their faith in him.

DAY 11

Read: Romans 4:1–25.

Reflect: Abraham was almost 100 years old when Isaac was born. His wife, Sarah, was so old that Paul writes her "womb was dead" (verse 19). Yet still, as Abraham advanced in age, he believed God's promise that he and Sarah would have a child of their own. How much trust in God does that take! What is a place in your life that your faith is wavering? How can you grow in faith as you trust God in this specific area?

Journal:
- What do you learn from the example of Abraham in Romans 4?
- How has God been faithful in your past? How can God's past faithfulness grow your confidence that he is trustworthy as you walk into the future?

Pray: Declare your faith and trust in Jesus as the resurrected and living Lord of your life.

DAY 12

Read: Romans 5:1–11.

Reflect: When we place our faith in Jesus, he justifies us. God Almighty grips us by his grace . . . and he will never let go. This should lead us to a place of abiding and profound peace. Even in times of suffering, we can live with hope and peace. Reflect on what Jesus has done to offer his peace to you. Take a deep breath (literally, do that right now) because the God of peace loves you and is with you. What moments of life and what experiences tend to help you experience God's grace?

Journal:
- What has God done for you through the life, death, and resurrection of Jesus? Why should knowing and believing this give you growing confidence and peace?
- Where are you facing hardship, pain, and suffering in your life right now? How can a growing sense of God's hand in your life help you walk

through this season of struggle with a clear sense of peace and hope?

Pray: Ask the Holy Spirit of the living God to deepen your peace and confidence in his grace and love for you.

DAY 13

Read: Romans 5:12–21.

Reflect: We have all received gifts from friends and family members. But the *greatest* gift ever given is the grace of God revealed in Jesus Christ. Take time to reflect on how the gift of Jesus is unique and different than every other gift you have received. (Think of the value of the gift, its enduring nature, and the perfection of Jesus.) How would you compare the grace of Jesus to the best birthday present you have ever received?

Journal:

- As you read this passage in Romans 5, notice that the world *gift* is used five times. What do you learn about this gift? Why is it so life-changing?
- We all have people we love who have not yet received God's good gifts. Who are a few of these people in your life? How can you pray for them to receive the amazing gift Jesus came to give them?

Pray: Pray for the people in your life who have not yet received the amazing, life-giving, eternity-changing gift of Jesus. Ask the Lord of the harvest if there is any next step you can take to share his love and grace with the people you have listed.

DAY 14

Memorize: Conclude this week's personal study by again reciting Romans 3:23–24:

> *For all have sinned and fall short of the glory of God, and all are justified freely by his grace through the redemption that came by Christ Jesus.*

Now try to say these verses completely from memory.

Reflect: What did the God the Father know about you when he sent his Son to die on the cross for you? (Be specific.) What does this tell you about God's love and your value to him?

THE BATTLE WE FIGHT

ROMANS 6–8

*Children of God who cry out, "Abba, Daddy,"
are still in a battle. Old patterns of life still entice us,
and the enemy of our soul still lies, steals, and seeks to
destroy us. Yet in all of this, we can know that
God has won the war, we are loved by him, and we
are more than conquerors!*

WELCOME

It was shocking! She was a Hollywood movie star with great wealth, masses of adoring fans, and producers lining up to hire her for their movies—and she had been arrested. What did she do? Was it drug use due to the pressures of the Hollywood scene? No. Was it a DUI after a night of celebrating her winning another award? No. She had been arrested for shoplifting. When the dust settled, it became clear that this young woman was stealing things she could have bought with her pocket change. Some things just don't make sense.

It was shocking! Another superstar athlete was bankrupt. He had earned millions upon millions. After years of exorbitant contracts to play a game he loved, he had less than nothing. Years of massive checks for endorsements and commercials were not enough. Now he owed more in taxes than he had in the bank. It is hard to imagine how he ended up where he did.

It is shocking! God has extended amazing grace. He sent his only Son to offer forgiveness and make us his children. He crushed the power of sin and hell under his heel. He cleansed us of sin and took our hand to lead us every day of our life. Yet, we wander back into the muck and mire of our old ways and sinful patterns. Instead of walking in confident freedom, if we are not careful, we could find ourselves crawling back into bed with the enemy. It makes no sense, but this is a battle all of us believers face.

SHARE

All three of the scenarios in the introduction are true stories of real people. Why are we so often shocked when we hear stories like these that seem to make no sense at all?

WATCH

Watch the video for session three. (Play the DVD or see the instructions on the inside front cover on how to access the sessions through streaming.) As you watch, use the following outline to record any thoughts or concepts that stand out to you.

What Jesus did to set us free

A story about a law-breaking pastor (Romans 6:6–7, 20–23)

The civil war that can rage in our soul (Romans 7:14–25)

When the battle rages:

Remember your *position*: you are a child of God (Romans 8:14–17)

Remember your *companion*: God still guides you (Romans 7:7–12)

Two great theological terms:

Positional sanctification (Hebrews 10:14)

Progressive sanctification (Romans 7:25)

One last piece of good news: no condemnation!

DISCUSS

Take a few minutes with your group members to discuss what you just watched and explore these concepts in Scripture. Use the following questions to help guide your discussion.

1. What impacted you the most as you watched Max's teaching on Romans 6–8?

2. **Read Romans 6:1–4.** Think about a time you accidently (or knowingly) broke the rules and, over time, eventually became comfortable with this pattern of behavior. When temptation comes, why it is so easy to rationalize our actions in this way?

3. **Read Romans 7:14–20.** Paul loved Jesus, had sound belief, and was a mature leader in the church. He wanted to do good, yet he still had moments when he struggled with doing things contrary to God's will. How can you relate to Paul's plight?

4. What does it mean to say that God is your heavenly Father and you are his child? Why is it essential to remember this when you are struggling with temptation and sin?

5. Back in the garden of Eden, the enemy of our soul used these words to deceive Eve: "Did God really say?" (Genesis 3:1). One of his most effective tactics today is still to get us to question the authority of God's Word in our lives. What are some of the ways that you have seen Satan employ these tactics? How can we fight against his enticements?

6. Read Romans 8:1–2 and 13–15. What is promised in these two passages? Why should these words bring you lasting hope and confidence as we fight the battle against the enemy and keep following Jesus?

MEMORIZE

Your memory verses for this week are from Romans 6:22–23:

But now that you have been set free from sin and have become slaves of God, the benefit you reap leads to holiness, and the result is eternal life. For the wages of sin is death, but the gift of God is eternal life in Christ Jesus our Lord.

Have everyone recite these verses out loud. Then go around the room again and have everyone try to say the verses completely from memory.

RESPOND

As noted in this week's teaching, progressive salvation is the idea that we are becoming more like Jesus with each passing day. What is a specific area of your life in which you feel led to pray and take action that will make you more like Jesus? How can your group members encourage and support you as you take these steps forward in becoming more like Christ?

PRAY

Close your group time by praying in any of the following directions:

- Thank Jesus for all he did to set you free. Give him praise for all he continues to do to empower you to live in victory.

- Ask the Holy Spirit to remind you, day after day, to live with the understanding that you are a child of God and led by him.
- Lift up praises that you are a child of the mighty God and that nothing can separate you from the love of God that you have in Christ.

SESSION THREE

Reflect on the material you have covered in this session by engaging in the following between-session learning resources. Each week, you will begin with a day to preview the biblical theme from the session. During the next five days, you will have an opportunity to read a portion of Romans, reflect on what you learn, respond by taking action, journal some of your insights, and pray about what God has taught you. Finally, on the last day, you will review the epic theme of the session, reflect on what you have learned, and review how it has impacted your life.

DAY 15

Memorize: Begin this week's personal study by reciting Romans 6:22–23:

> But now that you have been set free from sin and have become slaves of God, the benefit you reap leads to holiness, and the result is eternal life. For the wages of sin is death, but the gift of God is eternal life in Christ Jesus our Lord.

Now try to say these verses completely from memory.

Reflect: What is one specific area in your life in which you *desire* to do good but can't seem to *act* on it? What steps can you take in the coming days to do this one good thing?

DAY 16

Read: Romans 6:1–23.

Reflect: There are a number of ways to say *no* in Greek (the language of the New Testament). Sometimes, there is an implied *no* when you read a passage in English. In the first verse of Romans 6, we find a question that has such an implied *no* in the strongest negative in the Greek language. When Paul asks, "Shall we go on sinning so that grace may increase?" (verse 1), the built-in response is, "May it never be so!" or, "May God forbid it!" Why do you think Paul implies such a strong and clear *no* to this question he asks?

Journal:

- Some in the early church had adopted a mindset that said, "When I sin, I get grace. Grace is good. So, the more I sin, the more grace I get!" How would you describe the deceptive and twisted thinking behind this view of sin and grace? What are some situations where you have found yourself rationalizing something you knew was sinful because you also knew that God would still forgive you if you did it?

• When you find yourself preparing to rationalize an attitude of sin, sinful words, or sinful actions, what are some ways you can declare, "May it never be so!"?

Pray: Invite the Holy Spirit to convict you any time you begin to rationalize your sin.

DAY 17

Read: Romans 7:1–6.

Reflect: Each day we have a choice. We can choose to bear fruit for God or we can go back to bearing fruit for death. Jesus died for us and set us free so that we can live for him, serve him, and be fruitful for his glory. Reflect on where you have been fruitful in your walk with Jesus over the past month and invite God to bear even more fruit through you.

What fruit-bearing activity do you sense that God wants you to engage in today?

Journal:
- What are a few ways that you believe God wants to bear fruit in you?
- Circle the one you believe God wants you to take action on right away. What specific actions will you take to begin bearing fruit in this area?

Pray: Ask for the power of the Holy Spirit to be unleashed in you so that you can take action in one or more of these areas where God wants you to bear more fruit.

DAY 18

Read: Romans 7:7–25.

Reflect: After Paul pours out his honest confession that there were times he did the very things he hated, he broke into spontaneous praise to the God who had delivered him. As you look at your own life, why is it so important to keep praising God even when you are in a season where you are battling against sin and temptation?

Journal:
- What are some reasons you can praise God even during difficult times in your life?
- Write down three or four brief prayers of praise for ways that God has been with you and led you through these times of great difficulty.

Pray: Thank God, your great deliverer, that he is with you both in the best times in life and in the most challenging times of life.

DAY 19

Read: Romans 8:1–17.

Reflect: We live in a world filled with condemnation. We condemn ourselves, other people condemn us, and the enemy of our souls is constantly looking for ways to bring condemnation on us. Yet when we live and walk in Jesus, we find there is *no condemnation*. What are some indicators in your life that you are feeling condemned? How do you know when you are living free from condemnation?

Journal:
- What are some sources of condemnation that you have personally faced? How can Paul's words in Romans 8:1 empower you to resist these lies and hold to the truth?
- Write these words in capital letters over the words of condemnation that you have written: "THERE IS NO CONDEMNATION FOR ME!" What does

it mean for you that Jesus has set you free from these sources of condemnation in your life?

Pray: Thank Jesus for setting you free from all condemnation. Ask him to remind you of this truth every time anyone tries to heap condemnation on you.

DAY 20

Read: Romans 8:18–39.

Reflect: Near the end of this passage, the Holy Spirit inspired Paul to write, "We are more than conquerors through him who loved us" (Romans 8:37). Paul could have written, "We *are* conquerors." But the word *more* raises the bar. We are not just conquerors. We are *more* than conquerors! This is an amazing statement when you consider all of the things that Paul lists we are *more than conquerors* over—trouble, hardships, persecution, famine, nakedness, danger and sword (see verses 35–39). How do you respond to this idea that you are *more* than a conqueror in Christ over all these things?

Journal:

- In Jesus, you can walk in conquering victory! What are some of the things that Jesus has empowered you to conquer today?
- What are some specific areas where you have been giving in to temptation? What step can you take to fight back and live as more than a conqueror?

Pray: Thank Jesus for his victory. Pray for the power of the Holy Spirit to fill you so that you can live as more than a conqueror in the areas where you are feeling defeated.

DAY 21

Memorize: Conclude this week's personal study by again reciting Romans 6:22–23:

> *But now that you have been set free from sin and have become slaves of God, the benefit you reap leads to holiness, and the result is eternal life. For the wages of sin is death, but the gift of God is eternal life in Christ Jesus our Lord.*

Now try to say these verses completely from memory.

Reflect: What bold actions would you take for Christ if you lived with absolute conviction you had been set free from sin and nothing could separate you from God's love?

THE STORY WE'VE JOINED

ROMANS 9–11

The sixty-six books of our Bible tell a powerful, honest, and shocking story of God's work through ordinary and broken people. God is still writing this story, and every person who comes to the Father through faith in Jesus is part of this great drama that is unfolding.

WELCOME

Clive Staples Lewis was an academic. He taught at both Oxford and Cambridge universities in England. He had a brilliant mind and a wry sense of humor. Learning and teaching were his passion, and English literature was his expertise. Yet this gifted scholar decided to write a series of children's books about a magic land, talking animals, children who became royalty, and a giant lion named Aslan, who died and came back to life to offer salvation to his people.

C. S. Lewis understood the power of story. He recognized that he, along with the rest of humanity, had been swept into a great and epic drama that was still unfolding. The seven books that make up *The Chronicles of Narnia* were the result of his efforts to help both children and adults get a fresh perspective on some of the central themes of this epic story from God.

In this section of Romans, we find the apostle Paul doing something similar for his readers. He points backward, to the time of the Old Testament, to help the people in his day (and in ours) see the story of God. The biblical story does not have talking animals (aside from a snake and a donkey) but is filled with real people who encountered God, made their fair share of mistakes, and still held the hand of their creator through it all.

Paul recognized that he had joined this great story. In the first part, revealed in the Old Testament, God had promised to send a Savior into the world. In the second part, the age in which Paul was living, that Savior had arrived in Jesus. He was God in the flesh. Salvation was now available to all who put their trust in him—and with it the hope of eternal life.

God's desire today is still to sweep us into his arms, into his family, and into his story. He has a plan for each one of us. When we come to recognize this plan, all the random pieces of our lives come together, and everything begins to make sense.

SHARE

Think about a book or story (perhaps from the Bible) that has helped you make sense of your faith and God's plan for your life. What made that book or story so meaningful?

WATCH

Watch the video for session four. (Play the DVD or see the instructions on the inside front cover on how to access the sessions through streaming.) As you watch, use the following outline to record any thoughts or concepts that stand out to you.

Two big and sturdy tent poles (Romans 9:4–5)

God's chosen people: What does this mean? (Romans 9:6–9)

God's good gifts are given, never earned (Romans 9:10–26)

A close look at the family tree and why this is so important (Romans 11:1–10)

God chooses people for a divine purpose (Romans 11:11–16)

Believe in Jesus and be grafted into God's family (Romans 11:17–24)

DISCUSS

Take a few minutes with your group members to discuss what you just watched and explore these concepts in Scripture. Use the following questions to help guide your discussion.

1. What impacted you the most as you watched Max's teaching on Romans 9–11?

2. Just like the people of Israel, we will all encounter bumps and detours on our journey of faith. But God's plans never fail. In the end, he will accomplish his will in and through the lives of his people. When was a time you saw God

accomplish his will in your life or through your life, even though the road was a bit bumpy?

3. God blessed Abraham so he could be a conduit of heavenly blessings to all the nations of the world (see Genesis 12:3). What are some ways that God has used you to pour out his blessings to your family, your circle of friends, and your church or small group?

4. **Read Romans 10:1–4.** Paul's heart broke for his own people who had rejected the Messiah. He would have done anything to see them embrace the love and grace of Jesus. Think about a family member or loved one who has not yet received the amazing grace that God offers in Jesus. What would you do, give up, or risk to see that person enter a life-transforming relationship with him? How can your group members pray as you seek to help this person encounter Jesus?

5. **Read Romans 10:9–13.** The people of Israel saw themselves as different, distinct, and, in many cases, better than the other nations of the earth. How did God seek to correct their thinking? Why was it absolutely essential for God's people to recognize that Jesus offers himself to *everyone* with the same generous and gracious spirit?

6. **Read Romans 11:33–36.** Paul here breaks into passionate praise. Why does knowing the story of Jesus and recognizing our part in his story move our hearts and lips to praise? Describe the praise and thankfulness you are feeling right now after taking this time to focus on the story of God's amazing grace through history and in your life. .

MEMORIZE

Your memory verses for this week are from Romans 10:12–13:

For there is no difference between Jew and Gentile—the same Lord is Lord of all and richly blesses all who call on him, for, "Everyone who calls on the name of the Lord will be saved."

Have everyone recite these verses out loud. Then go around the room again and have everyone try to say the verses completely from memory.

RESPOND

In Romans 11:33–36, the apostle Paul breaks into Spirit-led praise and celebration of the goodness of God. He writes:

> *Oh, the depth of the riches of the wisdom and knowledge of God!*
> *How unsearchable his judgments,*
> *and his paths beyond tracing out!*
> *"Who has known the mind of the Lord?*
> *Or who has been his counselor?"*
> *"Who has ever given to God,*
> *that God should repay them?"*
> *For from him and through him and for him are all things.*
> *To him be the glory forever! Amen.*

What have you learned this week that will likewise lead you to praise God with prayers, songs, and spontaneous worship? In light of what you have learned in this session, what is one specific praise that is on your heart right now? Take a few moments to write down your thoughts.

PRAY

Close your group time by praying in any of the following directions:

- Thank God for giving you his Word. Express your appreciation to God for giving you both the Old and New Testaments and for how they bring a united message about the greatness of God's grace.
- Express to God your appreciation for calling you his child. Ask him to show you how he has blessed you so that you can be a blessing to others.
- Pray for those you love who are not yet gripped by the grace of God. Ask the Holy Spirit to open their eyes to see God's love and the gift Jesus offers them.

SESSION FOUR

Reflect on the material you have covered in this session by engaging in the following between-session learning resources. Each week, you will begin with a day to preview the biblical theme from the session. During the next five days, you will have an opportunity to read a portion of Romans, reflect on what you learn, respond by taking action, journal some of your insights, and pray about what God has taught you. Finally, on the last day, you will review the epic theme of the session, reflect on what you have learned, and review how it has impacted your life.

DAY 22

Memorize: Begin this week's personal study by reciting Romans 10:12–13:

> *For there is no difference between Jew and Gentile—the same Lord is Lord of all and richly blesses all who call on him, for, "Everyone who calls on the name of the Lord will be saved."*

Now try to say these verses completely from memory.

Reflect: What is required on your part to receive God's salvation? How do you respond to the fact that God offers his salvation freely . . . and to everyone?

DAY 23

Read: Romans 9:1–29.

Reflect: God is not only the Creator of all things, but he is also the sustainer and ruler of everything and everyone. In his infinite wisdom, God knows what is best for us and for all nations of the world. Rather than feeling threatened or bothered by God's sovereign power, we should celebrate it. Only God can take rebellious, stubborn people and soften their hearts to become loving children. Think back over your personal journey to faith in Jesus. Reflect on your walk with him as a beloved child. Then, celebrate the glimpses you have seen of his sovereign hand moving on your behalf. What is one way God has protected, provided, or been present with you through a hard time over the past months?

Journal:
- How would you describe the heart of Paul for his own people and the depth of his desire to see them embrace Jesus as the Messiah and their Savior?
- Write down the names of people in your family and circle of friends who are still living far from Jesus. Write a heartfelt prayer for God to reach out to them and draw them to the grace of Jesus.

Pray: Thank God for loving you and drawing you to himself. Ask him to draw your loved ones, who have not yet found salvation in Christ, into his arms by his sovereign power.

DAY 24

Read: Romans 9:30–10:21.

Reflect: God does his part—only he can save. Only God was able to make a way for us to come home through the amazing grace of Jesus. It is the sacrifice of Jesus that makes forgiveness possible and friendship with God our inheritance. God did for us what we could never do for ourselves. At the same time, we are called to open our mouths and declare, "Jesus is Lord!" We also wrap our hearts around the truth that Jesus rose from the dead after dying for our sins. Salvation is offered by God, and it can be accepted by anyone who will humble themselves and cry out to Jesus. As you think about people in your life who are still far from Jesus, pray that they will open their mouth to declare and their heart to receive. What is one way you can begin a spiritual conversation with a friend or family member who still needs to receive the grace of Jesus?

Journal:
- How can you express your gratefulness for what God has done to save you and lavish you with his grace?
- What is your part in receiving his grace? How can you encourage others to open their hearts to receive, their minds to believe, and their mouths to declare that Jesus is Lord?

Pray: Ask God to give you insight, wisdom, and courage as you discover the best way to share the story of Jesus' grace with those in your life who need the truth that he offers.

DAY 25

Read: Romans 11:1–10.

Reflect: God is patient beyond your wildest imaginations. You might run from him and even reject him, but he remains faithful and will not reject you. As the apostle Paul writes, "Did God reject his people?" (Romans 11:1). His answer comes swiftly and decisively: "By no means!" Take time to reflect on how many times God could have turned his back on you and rejected you . . . but he did not. Then, lift up declarations of thanks and praise for God's astounding grace and determination to do all he can to save you from your sins. How can you run *toward* God in times of need rather than run *from* him in shame?

Journal:

- What were some of the ways the people of Israel rebelled and ran from God (see Psalm 106)? How did God love, discipline, and keep holding on to them?
- What are some of the ways *you* have rebelled and run from God? How has he lovingly and patiently gripped you by his grace and never let you go?

Pray: Thank God that you live in the grip of his grace every day. Praise him that, through faith in Jesus, you will always be his.

DAY 26

Read: Romans 11:11–24.

Reflect: Who is in the club? Who is welcome? Who has God invited into his "forever family"? The answer is clear: *you*! Whoever you are! Any person who places faith in Jesus and embraces his grace receives a heavenly welcome. In the days of the apostle Paul, there were many Jewish people who believed God only loved and chose *them*. There was a sense of exclusivity. Among some of the non-Jewish Christians, there was a sense of pride that they now belonged in God's family and had taken the place of Jewish people who had been persistent in their unbelief in Jesus the Messiah. But Paul made it clear that we are *all* welcome. There is no room for pride in the heart of anyone. It is God's grace that saves. What is one way you can extend a welcome to someone who is not yet part of God's family (such as a welcome to your church, a church event, your home, or just a welcome to be closer to you)?

Journal:
- Paul uses a powerful image of an olive tree, where some branches are cut off and others were grafted in. As you read this passage, write down what you see happening and why some branches (people) are added in and why others are cut off. What message is God seeking to teach us through this word-picture?

- What does it mean to be made a part of the family
of God—adopted and grafted in?

Pray: Thank Jesus for his sacrifice to bring you into his family. Pray for a humble heart that always recognizes God has reached out to you, loved you, and made you his own.

DAY 27

Read: Romans 11:25–36.

Reflect: At the close of this portion of Romans, the apostle Paul is moved to a glorious declaration of praise to the Lord. His words in Romans 11:33–36 celebrate the sovereignty of God. As you read them, think about who God is and the greatness of his wisdom, judgments, paths, and mind. Pray these words out loud and make them the declaration of your heart. How can you share this beautiful prayer with someone else in your life (type and send it, post it somewhere, or lead someone in this prayer)?

Journal:
- Write down each declaration of God's sovereignty listed in Romans 11:33–36. How do these declarations point to the glorious nature of our God?
- Think about the words, "To him be the glory forever" (verse 36). What are some ways you can show glory to God today—and every day?

Pray: Ask the Holy Spirit to help you live in humility under the sovereign hand of God. Pray that you will increasingly learn to trust all that he does on your behalf.

DAY 28

Memorize: Conclude this week's personal study by again reciting Romans 10:12–13:

> For there is no difference between Jew and Gentile—the same Lord is Lord of all and richly blesses all who call on him, for, "Everyone who calls on the name of the Lord will be saved."

Now try to say these verses completely from memory.

Reflect: Who in your life needs to "call on the name of the Lord" and receive salvation? How will you pray for that person and show them the grace of Jesus in the coming days?

THE PATH WE FOLLOW

ROMANS 12–13

*To walk in the footsteps of Jesus is to walk in love.
To become more like Jesus is to love others more freely.
When we receive the agape love of God, it overflows to
every person we encounter!*

WELCOME

Have you ever played the party game called "Two Truths and a Lie"? The simple concept is that each person declares three things about his or her life experience. Two are true, while one is not. The others in the group then guess which one of the three declarations is not true.

"I have never had a cup of coffee. I have had only one cavity my entire life. I love jazz music. Tell me, which is not true?"

"I can juggle three balls at the same time. I am double jointed in both my arms. I know all the US states and capitals. You tell me, which is not true?"

You get the idea. It's just a way of sharing fun and random information, but the truth always reveals part of a person's story. The more we know the truth *about* a person, the more we know who they truly are *as* a person. In the same way, in Romans 12–13, God unfolds the truth about those who follow his Son. As he does, we come to discover the truth about ourselves now and the truth about the people we are becoming.

Imagine that you are using Romans 12–13 as your source for what is true about you. As you begin to read, you quickly discover:

- Your life is a sacrifice pleasing to God.
- When you surrender to God, it is an act of worship.
- Your mind is being renewed by God.
- You can know and follow the will of the living God.
- You have been given grace.
- You are called to humility and to think with sober judgment.
- You belong to God's family, his Church.
- You are gifted by God.

Those truths are found in just the first six verses of Romans 12. There is a lot more to learn. So read on! And if anyone asks you to play "Two Truths and a Lie," maybe you can look at the list of truths from the book of Romans for your truth statements.

SHARE

What is one true thing about you that might be surprising for your group members to know?

WATCH

Watch the video for session five. (Play the DVD or see the instructions on the inside front cover on how to access the sessions through streaming.) As you watch, use the following outline to record any thoughts or concepts that stand out to you.

The start of the path: receiving the gift of grace (Romans 12:1)

Stand against the patterns of this world as you offer your whole life to God (Romans 12:2)

The contrast between how rulers in Rome saw themselves (authority, power, and pride) and how followers of Jesus should view themselves (service and humility) (Romans 12:3–8)

We can't give what we don't have: we must receive God's *agape* love (John 3:16)

God's love for us is lavish and we should follow his example (Romans 12:9–21)

People who really need God's love through you: pray for a new attitude

DISCUSS

Take a few minutes with your group members to discuss what you just watched and explore these concepts in Scripture. Use the following questions to help guide your discussion.

1. What impacted you the most as you watched Max's teaching on Romans 12–13?

2. **Read Romans 12:1.** The world entices us to a life of self-indulgence, self-expression, and self-celebration, but Jesus invites us to a life of meekness, humility, and sacrificial love. What are indicators that a person is following the path of the world with "self" at the center of everything? What are signs that a person is seeking to walk the path of Jesus—with meekness, humility, and sacrificial love?

3. **Read Romans 12:3–5.** What picture does this passage paint of the heart of a Jesus follower? What picture does it paint regarding our relationship to other Christians? What would the church look like if we all truly followed this vision for our lives?

4. **Read Romans 13:8–10.** How can the simple command to love others be the fulfillment of all the biblical commands? How does loving like Jesus move us to live in ways that can change the world around us?

5. What are some of the dangers and problems we will face if we try to love others in our power, by our motivation, and when we feel like it? What will happen if we simply receive God's love every day, in its fullness, and then let it overflow to others?

6. What are some biblical examples mentioned during the teaching of God pouring out lavish, abundant, rich goodness into the lives of his people? What is an example of a time that God lavished you with his love—and you really felt it?

MEMORIZE

Your memory verse for this week is from Romans 12:2:

Do not conform to the pattern of this world, but be transformed by the renewing of your mind. Then you will be able to test and approve what God's will is—his good, pleasing and perfect will.

Have everyone recite this verse out loud. Then go around the room again and have everyone try to say the verse completely from memory.

RESPOND

Who is one person you find challenging to love? What is a step forward on the pathway of agape love that you believe God wants you to take toward this person? Write down one or two actions you can take in the coming week that will move you toward agape love in this relationship and that will also let the person experience this love from God and you.

PRAY

Close your group time by praying in any of the following directions:

- Commit to offer your whole life—all you are—as a living sacrifice for the glory of God. Pray for the courage to place your whole life on the altar and surrender all you are to Jesus.

- Pray for God to give you a deeper understanding of his agape love for you. Ask for a clear awareness of how you are loved. Pray that this love from God will flow through you to every person you meet.

- Ask God to help you (and your group members) express love with growing authenticity to those people in your life who are hard to love.

SESSION FIVE

Reflect on the material you have covered in this session by engaging in the following between-session learning resources. Each week, you will begin with a day to preview the biblical theme from the session. During the next five days, you will have an opportunity to read a portion of Romans, reflect on what you learn, respond by taking action, journal some of your insights, and pray about what God has taught you. Finally, on the last day, you will review the epic theme of the session, reflect on what you have learned, and review how it has impacted your life.

DAY 29

Memorize: Begin this week's personal study by reciting Romans 12:2:

> Do not conform to the pattern of this world, but be transformed by the renewing of your mind. Then you will be able to test and approve what God's will is—his good, pleasing and perfect will.

Now try to say the verse completely from memory.

Reflect: When you receive God's love, how should it transform your attitudes and actions?

DAY 30

Read: Romans 12:1–8.

Reflect: Body imagery is used in two ways in this portion of Romans 12. First, we are called to offer our bodies—a picture of all we are—to God. This is about full surrender. Then, we learn we are part of a living spiritual body called the Church. We are each connected and belong to each other. Here is the picture: (1) offer your body to Jesus, fully and with no reservations; and then (2) fully engage as a part of the living body of Jesus, his family, the Church. What is your next step to fully surrendering to God's plan for your life? How can you serve and love others more faithfully within the local church where God has placed you?

Journal:

- What does it look like when you (personally) are fully engaged in the life of the church, the body of Jesus? How do you know when you are drifting and not fully functioning as part of the body of Jesus?
- What is your next step to engage more meaningfully in your church? Do you need to pray more, love more, give more, serve more, or take some other step into full engagement in the life of your church? Explain.

Pray: Pray for the leaders of your local church. Ask for God's blessing and protection in their lives. Lift up their needs. If you are not sure how to pray for them, dare to ask!

DAY 31

Read: Romans 12:9–21.

Reflect: Most every home has a drawer where they keep odds and ends—rubber bands, paper clips, pencils, a few AAA batteries, and the like. Some call it the "junk drawer," others the "knick-knack drawer," and others just know where it is. This passage is the Bible's version of that kind of drawer. But what fills this drawer are the *good things* that followers of Jesus will do when they are receiving and sharing the agape love of God. It is like a rapid-fire barrage of reminders of what our lives can look like when we follow the path of Jesus. Reflect on one action mentioned that you are doing well and lift up a prayer of celebration. What is one area you need to pray about and ask God to give you strength to follow this path of Jesus?

Journal:
- What are five actions in this passage that you know God wants you to take as a next step forward in your growth?
- What one or two actions will you take to go deeper in this area of growth?

Pray: Ask the Holy Spirit to shine the light and presence of Jesus through the action you are going to take in the coming days.

DAY 32

Read: Romans 13:1–7.

Reflect: We like to follow rules and regulations when we agree with them. We are good with submitting to leaders we respect and trust. But it's more difficult to follow the rules and the rulers we don't like. In the first century, there were plenty of political leaders who were not friendly toward the church. Some were downright brutal with Christians. How do you follow the exhortations in this passage when you don't trust or like the leaders? How do Christians maintain their witness while still being distinctively Christian in an increasingly secular world?

Journal:
- How do you balance your view of the sovereignty of God with the call to honor and be subject to governing authorities?

• What is a specific way you could honor, bless, or encourage some of the governing authorities in your community?

Pray: Pray for some of the community leaders and people in government in your local area and your state (even if you don't agree with them politically).

DAY 33

Read: Romans 13:8–10.

Reflect: Christians are to live with only one debt: *to love one another.* The context of this passage is the Ten Commandments (in particular, the commands about how we relate to other people). Think of it this way. Every day, when you wake up, you could think, "I have a debt to pay. I am to love the people I encounter!" If you lived this way, you would look at the people around your dining room table with fresh eyes on how to love them. When you got cut off on the road, you would think, "I owe some love . . . how can I show it right now?" Your friends (and even strangers) are opportunities to invest some loving actions, words, and attitudes. So, who can you love in words and actions in the next twenty-four hours? In what ways can you show love to those individuals?

Journal:

- How can living with persistent and Jesus-motivated love fulfill the Ten Commandments mentioned in this passage?
- Who is one person you feel does not *deserve* love from you? Think about three or four ways you could show love to this person. Write down how you feel that person might see Jesus if you dared to act on a couple of those ideas.

Pray: Ask God to give you courage to initiate specific actions of love toward one person you tend to avoid.

DAY 34

Read: Romans 13:11–14.

Reflect: In this passage, Paul talks about the "deeds of darkness" (verse 12). He tells us to avoid these sinful actions and expose them to God's light. What are some of the behaviors that Paul lists that belong to these deeds of darkness?

Journal:
- What does it mean to "put on the armor of light" (verse 12)? How can you live and walk in God's light so you are less likely to engage in the behaviors that Paul lists?
- What is one way you can shed light on an area of your life where you are tempted to live in dark ways? (Consider contacting a trusted Christian friend, asking them to pray for you in this area, and potentially asking them for accountability.)

Pray: Ask God to help you walk in the light and avoid spiritually dark places.

DAY 35

Memorize: Conclude this week's personal study by reciting Romans 12:2:

> *Do not conform to the pattern of this world, but be transformed by the renewing of your mind. Then you will be able to test and approve what God's will is—his good, pleasing and perfect will.*

Now try to say the verse completely from memory.

Reflect: How can you worship God with greater devotion in the coming week by offering more of your life, dreams, and plans on the altar of his amazing grace?

THE FELLOWSHIP WE FIND

ROMANS 14–16

Every Christian is part of God's family. God delights when his people are united and walk in the spirit of love. But fellowship is a fragile thing, and the enemy of our souls loves to rock the boat. So, if we are going to honor God and build a church that shows his glory to the world, we must do all we can to bring unity, grace, and peace to the family of God.

WELCOME

When it comes to creating health, stability, and unity in an institution, it can take years, huge amounts of effort, and intentional sacrifice on the part of its members to reach that state. On the other hand, it only takes a few moments to cause division, sow seeds of conflict, and create disunity.

With one bad decision, harsh word, or thoughtless action, division can erupt.

It is so much easier to divide than to unite. This is true in a home, marriage, workplace, friendship . . . and certainly in a church. God delights in the fellowship and unity of his people. The enemy, on the other hand, delights when he can stir up conflict, arguments, and division.

Most pastors could write a book titled *101 Ways to Divide a Church*. Sadly, all too many Christian leaders have witnessed the tactics of the enemy causing untold pain and conflict among their members. Just imagine this table of contents:

- **Chapter 1:** Carpet, Decorations, and Stylistic Squabbles
- **Chapter 2:** Drums, Music Style, and "What Blesses Me"
- **Chapter 3:** Board Meetings, Congregational Meetings, and Committee Meetings
- **Chapter 4:** Sermon Length, Preaching Style, and Politics in the Pulpit
- **Chapter 5:** Pet Peeves, Pet Projects, and Pets in the Pews

There are endless things that can divide a church—and only one that can hold it all together. His name is *Jesus*. When we are gripped by his grace and walking in his ways, humility grows in the church and community becomes possible. But if we demand our own way, cling to preferences, major on the minors, and jettison grace, we might as well put up a sign in front of our church that reads: "FIRST CHURCH OF DIS-UNITY, CONFLICT, AND DIVISION."

SHARE

Think about a church conflict you saw or experienced. What events led to it happening? What did it cost the congregation and their witness in the community?

WATCH

Watch the video for session six. (Play the DVD or see the instructions on the inside front cover on how to access the sessions through streaming.) As you watch, use the following outline to record any thoughts or concepts that stand out to you.

Fellowship happens in imperfect churches (because that's the only kind of church there is)

Paul did not start the church in Rome, but he wanted to help the church thrive

A conflict in Rome: *to eat or not to eat?*

Various responses (Romans 14:1–9)

The deeper issue: division in the family of God (Romans 14:10–21)

Don't let trivial conflict damage the fellowship of the church (Romans 14:22–15:13)

The S.S. Fellowship is not a cruise ship but a battleship

The key to harmony: the example of Jesus

Can we have unity with Christians from other churches and traditions?

DISCUSS

Take a few minutes with your group members to discuss what you just watched and explore these concepts in Scripture. Use the following questions to help guide your discussion.

1. What impacted you the most as you watched Max's teaching on Romans 14–16?

2. **Read Romans 14:1–21.** What were some of the different ways the Christians in Rome responded to the idea of eating meat that might have been sacrificed to an idol? Why was each response a matter of personal conviction and choice?

3. Paul saw a deeper issue at hand. More than eating (or not eating) meat from the local markets, Paul was concerned about how this debate was damaging the fellowship in the church. How have you seen division in the church over different issues? What are some of the signs that a local church is heading into the rough waters of disunity?

4. Max says in his teaching, "The church is not a cruise ship; it is a battleship!" What are some of the consequences if members of the church see it as a cruise ship designed to meet their needs? What could we expect to see if members of the church all saw it as a battleship and were united in their mission, calling, and collaborative efforts?

5. **Read Romans 15:7 and John 13:34.** Jesus loved others and accepted them right where they were. What are some ways you can do the same sort of things in your relationships with people both inside and outside of the church?

6. **Read Romans 16:20.** We are in a battle and have a very real enemy. Our enemy is *not* other Bible-believing and Jesus-loving Christians. These people are shipmates and fellow soldiers. We are in a spiritual battle, and God is ready to crush the work of Satan as we stand united. What are a few ways your small group can pray, serve, and engage in your local church in a way that will lead to unity and healthy fellowship?

MEMORIZE

Your memory verse for this final week is from Romans 15:7:

Accept one another, then, just as Christ accepted you, in order to bring praise to God.

Have everyone recite the verse out loud. Then go around the room again and have everyone try to say the verse completely from memory.

RESPOND

Think about a lesson you learned or the way God blessed and formed you through a Christian who came from a tradition other than your own. (You might have met the person face to face, listened to a message online, read a book they wrote, or been influenced in some other way.) What lesson or blessing did you receive from that person? How can unity with Christians of various backgrounds actually strengthen your faith and expand your witness to the world?

PRAY

Close your group time by praying in any of the following directions:

- Ask God to give you insight where you might be operating in freedom, but your liberty is causing other believers to struggle and stumble. Ask the Spirit to show you what you should do (or not do) to be a blessing to those people.
- Confess where you have been a source of division or disunity in your church or community. Ask for forgiveness and a repentant heart. Then pray that you will no longer be a source of conflict as you move forward.
- Pray for God to lead you to such profound unity with other believers that the world will look on and see that God is near, caring, and at work for all.

SESSION SIX

Reflect on the material you have covered in this session by engaging in the following learning resources. You will begin with a day to preview the biblical theme from the session. During the next five days, you will have an opportunity to read a portion of Romans, reflect on what you learn, respond by taking action, journal some of your insights, and pray about what God has taught you. Finally, on the last day, you will review the epic theme of the session, reflect on what you have learned, and review how it has impacted your life.

DAY 36

Memorize: Begin this week's personal study by reciting Romans 15:7:

Accept one another, then, just as Christ accepted you, in order to bring praise to God.

Now try to say this verse completely from memory.

Reflect: What is required on your part to accept others just as Jesus has accepted you?

DAY 37

Read: Romans 14:1–15:13.

Reflect: God delights in unity, harmony, and healthy relationships between Christians. It breaks his heart to see his children squabbling and arguing over things that really don't matter. In the ancient world, dietary regulations were a point of conflict for some people. What are some of the peripheral issues that divide believers in your church tradition or congregation? What can you do to be about unity more than division?

Journal:
- What were some of the various perspectives about eating meat in Rome? Why were these diverse views becoming a source of conflict and disunity?

- What are some areas of diverse perspective today that are simply not worth fighting over or letting them divide us?

Pray: Thank God for the beautiful variety of people and outlooks that exist in the church.

DAY 38

Read: Romans 15:14–33.

Reflect: The apostle Paul was committed to keeping his eyes and heart fixed on Jesus. All his life, his plans, and his dreams were wrapped up in the Savior. What a powerful reminder for each of us! If our lives are all about Jesus, they will be on the right path, with the right attitude, and be doing the right things. What is one attitude adjustment you need to make? How can you work at this in the coming days?

Journal:
- How were Paul's eyes fixed on Jesus and his plans driven by the will of God? What can you learn from his example?
- What is one area of your life that is not properly aligned with the heart and will of Christ? What can you do to get things into better alignment?

Pray: Ask for courage to follow God's will and plan for your life, even when it is hard and others might not understand.

DAY 39

Read: Romans 16.

Reflect: Paul was all about people. He wanted them to know Jesus, love the Savior, and walk in the ways of God. In this final chapter of Romans, his care for people shines through. He is quick to offer them warm and personal greetings. He does not shy away from pointing out what people do well. He is always ready to encourage others to grow and go deeper in their faith and faithfulness to the Savior. Today, take time to reflect on a few Christians you know with whom you have not connected recently. Send them a text, an email, or give them a call. Just say hello, commend them for something in their life that honors Jesus, and encourage them to keep following Jesus and living in the light of his amazing grace. Record the response you received from this person and how it impacted you (you might want to use the space below). What can you do to make this a regular practice?

Journal:
- What words of greeting, kindness, and encouragement did Paul offer the people mentioned in this final chapter of Romans?
- Think of a church leader you know who "works hard in the Lord." What do you appreciate about this person's faith? How have they impacted you? Consider taking time to thank them for their example and impact on your faith.

Pray: Lift up a prayer of thanks to God for the people he has placed in your life who have strengthened your faith and revealed the grace of Jesus to you.

DAY 40

Memorize: Conclude your forty-day personal study by reciting Romans 15:7:

> *Accept one another, then, just as Christ accepted you, in order to bring praise to God.*

Now try to say this verse completely from memory.

Reflect: How have you experienced God's grace and acceptance as you have gone on this journey in Romans? How will this impact the way you share God's grace with others?

LEADER'S GUIDE

Thank you for your willingness to lead your group through this study! What you have chosen to do is valuable and will make a great difference in the lives of others. The rewards of being a leader are different from those of participating, and we hope that as you lead you will find your own walk with Jesus deepened by this experience.

This study on Romans in the *40 Days Through the Book* series is built around video content and small-group interaction. As the group leader, think of yourself as the host. Your job is to take care of your guests by managing the behind-the-scenes details so that when everyone arrives, they can enjoy their time together. As the leader, your role is not to answer all the questions or reteach the content—the video, book, and study guide will do that work. Your role is to guide the experience and cultivate your group into a teaching community. This will make it a place for members to process, question, and reflect on the teaching.

Before your first meeting, make sure everyone has a copy of the study guide. This will keep everyone on the same page and help the process run more smoothly. If members are unable to purchase the guide, arrange it so they can share with other members. Everyone should feel free to write in his or her study guide and bring it to group every week. Also, make sure the group members are aware that they have access to the videos at any time by following the instructions on the inside front cover.

SETTING UP THE GROUP

Your group will need to determine how long you want to meet each week so you can plan your time accordingly. Generally, most groups like to meet for either sixty minutes or ninety minutes, so you could use one of the following schedules:

SECTION	60 MINUTES	90 MINUTES
WELCOME (members arrive and get settled)	5 minutes	5 minutes
SHARE (discuss one or more of the opening questions for the session)	5 minutes	10 minutes
READ (discuss the questions based on the Scripture reading for the session)	5 minutes	10 minutes
WATCH (watch the video teaching material together and take notes)	15 minutes	15 minutes
DISCUSS (discuss the Bible study questions based on the video teaching)	25 minutes	40 minutes
RESPOND / PRAY (reflect on the key insights, pray together, and dismiss)	5 minutes	10 minutes

As the group leader, you will want to create an environment that encourages sharing and learning. A church sanctuary or formal classroom may not be as ideal as a living room, because those locations can feel formal and less intimate. No matter what setting you choose, provide enough comfortable seating for everyone, and, if possible, arrange the seats in a semicircle so everyone can see the video easily. This will make the transition between the video and group conversation more efficient and natural.

Also, try to get to the meeting site early so you can greet participants as they arrive. Simple refreshments create a welcoming atmosphere and can be a wonderful addition to a group study. Try to take food and pet allergies into account to make your guests as comfortable as possible. You may also want to consider offering childcare to couples with children who want to attend. Finally, be sure your media technology is working properly. Managing these details up front will make the rest of your group experience flow smoothly and provide a welcoming space in which to engage the content of this study on the book of Romans.

STARTING THE GROUP TIME

Once everyone has arrived, it is time to begin the study. Here are some simple tips to make your group time healthy, enjoyable, and effective.

Begin the meeting with a short prayer and remind the group members to put their phones on silent. This is a way to make sure you can all be present with one another and with God. Next, give each person a few minutes to respond to the questions in the "Share" section. This won't require as much time in session one, but beginning in session two, people may need more time to share their insights from their personal studies. Usually, you won't answer the discussion questions yourself, but you should go first with the "Share" questions, answering briefly and with a reasonable amount of transparency.

At the end of session one, invite the group members to complete the "Your 40-Day Journey" for that week. Explain that they can share any insights the following week before the video teaching. Let them know it's not a problem if they can't get to these activities some weeks. It will still be beneficial for them to hear from the other participants in the group.

LEADING THE DISCUSSION TIME

Now that the group is engaged, watch the video and respond with some directed small-group discussion. (Play the DVD or see the instructions on the inside front cover on how to access the sessions through streaming.) Encourage the group members to participate in the discussion, but make sure they know this is not mandatory for the group, so as to not make them feel pressured to come up with an answer. As the discussion progresses, follow up with comments such as, "Tell me more about that," or, "Why did you answer that way?" This will allow the group participants to deepen their reflections and invite a meaningful conversation in a nonthreatening way.

Note that you have been given multiple questions to use in each session, and you do not have to use them all or even follow them in order. Feel free to pick and choose questions based on the needs of your group or how the conversation is flowing. Also, don't be afraid of silence. Offering a question and allowing up to thirty seconds of silence is okay. This space allows people to think about how they want to respond and gives them time to do so.

As group leader, you are the boundary keeper for your group. Do not let anyone (yourself included) dominate the group time. Keep an eye out for group members who might be tempted to "attack" folks they disagree with or try to "fix" those having struggles. These kinds of behaviors can derail a group's momentum, so they need to be steered in a different direction. Model active listening and encourage everyone in your group to do the same. This will make your group time a safe space and create a positive community.

The group discussion leads to a closing time of individual reflection and prayer. Encourage the participants to review what they have learned and write down their thoughts in the "Respond" section. Close by taking a few minutes to pray as directed as a group.

Thank you again for taking the time to lead your group. You are making a difference in the lives of others and having an impact on the kingdom of God!

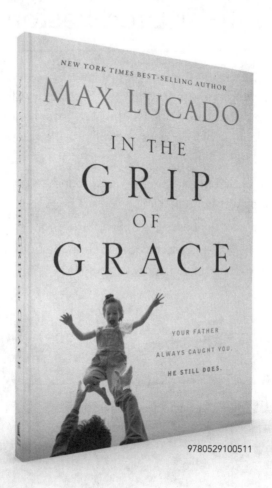

YOU BELIEVE JESUS IS **GOD.** BUT DO YOU ALSO THINK OF HIM AS A **REAL PERSON**?

In this book and video Bible study, Max Lucado reveals that because Jesus became human, it is now possible for us to see God and hear his voice. If we want to know what matters to God, all we need to do is look in the Bible to see what matters to Jesus. If we want to know what God is doing in our world, we need only ponder the words of Jesus. By learning more about the person Jesus was and is, we come to understand more clearly the people we were created to be.

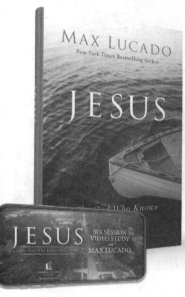
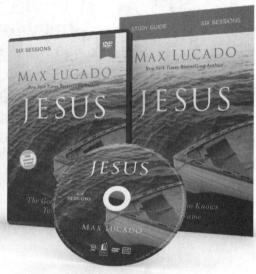

Book	Study Guide	DVD with Free Streaming Access
9781400214693	9780310105831	9780310105855

Available now at your favorite bookstore, or streaming video on StudyGateway.com.

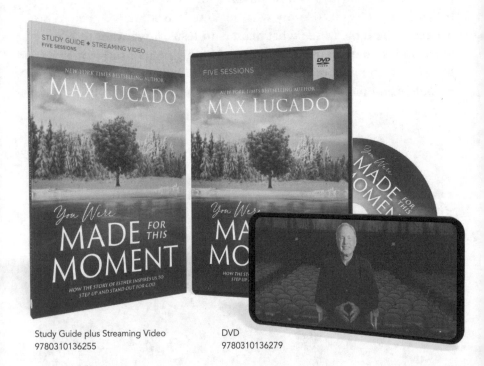

THERE IS A PATH TO HAPPINESS THAT ALWAYS DELIVERS

In this book and video Bible study, Max Lucado shares the unexpected path to a lasting happiness, one that produces reliable joy in any season of life. Based on the teachings of Jesus and backed by modern research, *How Happiness Happens* presents a surprising but practical way of living that will change you from the inside out.

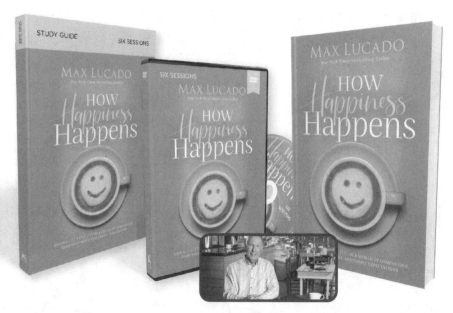

Study Guide
9780310105718

DVD with Free Streaming Access
9780310105732

Book
9780718096137

Available now at your favorite bookstore,
or streaming video on StudyGateway.com.

THOMAS NELSON
Since 1798

GOD HAS A CURE FOR YOUR WORRIES

Anxiety doesn't have to dominate life. Max looks at seven admonitions from the Apostle Paul in Philippians 4:4–8 that lead to one wonderful promise: "The peace of God which surpasses all understanding." He shows how God is ready to give comfort to help us face the calamities in life, view bad news through the lens of sovereignty, discern the lies of Satan, and tell ourselves the truth. We can discover true peace from God that surpasses all human understanding.

Study Guide	DVD	Softcover
9780310087311	9780310087335	9780718074210

Available now at your favorite bookstore,
or streaming video on StudyGateway.com.

STUDY THE BIBLE BOOK-BY-BOOK
WITH MAX LUCADO

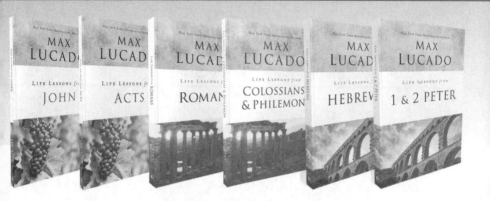

The *Life Lessons with Max Lucado* series brings the Bible to life in twelve lessons filled with intriguing questions, inspirational stories, and poignant reflections to take you deeper into God's Word. Each lesson includes an opening reflection, background information, an excerpt of the text, exploration questions, inspirational thoughts from Max, and a closing takeaway for further reflection. Ideal for use in both a small-group setting and for individual study.

9780310086741	Genesis	9780310086468	Galatians
9780310086703	Daniel & Esther	9780310086482	Ephesians
9780310086727	Ezra & Nehemiah	9780310086505	Philippians
9780310086680	Psalms	9780310086529	Colossians and Philemon
9780310086307	Matthew	9780310086543	1 and 2 Thessalonians
9780310086321	Mark	9780310086567	1 and 2 Timothy
9780310086345	Luke		and Titus
9780310086369	John	9780310086581	Hebrews
9780310086383	Acts	9780310086604	James
9780310086406	Romans	9780310086628	1 and 2 Peter
9780310086420	1 Corinthians	9780310086642	1, 2, 3 John and Jude
9780310086444	2 Corinthians	9780310086666	Revelation

Available now at your favorite bookstore.